GOATS
ON THE **FAMILY FARM**

Chana Stiefel

Enslow Elementary

an imprint of

Enslow Publishers, Inc.

40 Industrial Road
Box 398
Berkeley Heights, NJ 07922
USA

http://www.enslow.com

CONTENTS

WORDS TO KNOW

breed—One type of animal in a group.

buck—A male goat.

doe—A female goat.

herd—A group of goats.

hoof—A goat's toe.

kid—A baby goat.

yearling—A one-year-old goat.

PARTS OF A GOAT

horn

ear

eye

nose

mouth

beard

head

body

tail

leg

hoof

TREE
PICNIC

Did you know that goats can climb trees? They also like to eat stems and leaves. Read to find out more fun facts about goats on the family farm.

GOT GOATS?

Tara (with Alice in front), Matt, and Jack are ready for the day.

Matt and Tara raise goats on their family farm. They raise many other animals, too. Their children, Jack and Alice, help take care of the animals.

A group of goats is called a herd.

GOAT
FAMILY

A male goat is called a **buck** or billy. A female is called a **doe** or nanny. Baby goats are known as **kids**. A group of goats is a **herd**.

A newborn kid is about the size of a cat.

EATING MACHINES

Hay is dry grass. It is important food for goats in the winter.

Goats share the fields with cows. The goats eat and chew all day. They like bushes, buds, vines, and plant stems. They also eat grass and clover. The goats stay outside all year. In winter, Jack feeds them hay.

Goats spend the day eating lots of grass.

Goats might eat the bark off a tree.

SILLY EATERS

Goats are very curious. Sometimes they eat odd things. "They nibbled wood off the barn!" says Tara. She has to keep the goats away from her garden. They will eat her vegetables and flowers. The goats may even munch on poison ivy plants, but they are not harmed.

Goats nibble with their lips.

JUMP!

Goats' toes are called hooves. Wet hooves can lead to a disease called "foot rot." Matt and Tara make sure their goats graze in drier fields, away from wet, muddy ground.

Goats love to jump and climb. The hard part of the **hooves** protects the foot from sharp twigs and stones. The soft part helps goats leap onto rocks and climb trees. "I've seen goats jump over a five-foot fence!" says Matt.

This goat jumped onto a table!

15

GOAT
COATS

Goats come in many colors. They may be white, tan, gray, black, brown, or a mix. Bucks and does look alike, but bucks grow bigger. They both may have beards and horns. The does have udders to give milk.

The buck on the right is a bit bigger than the doe.

17

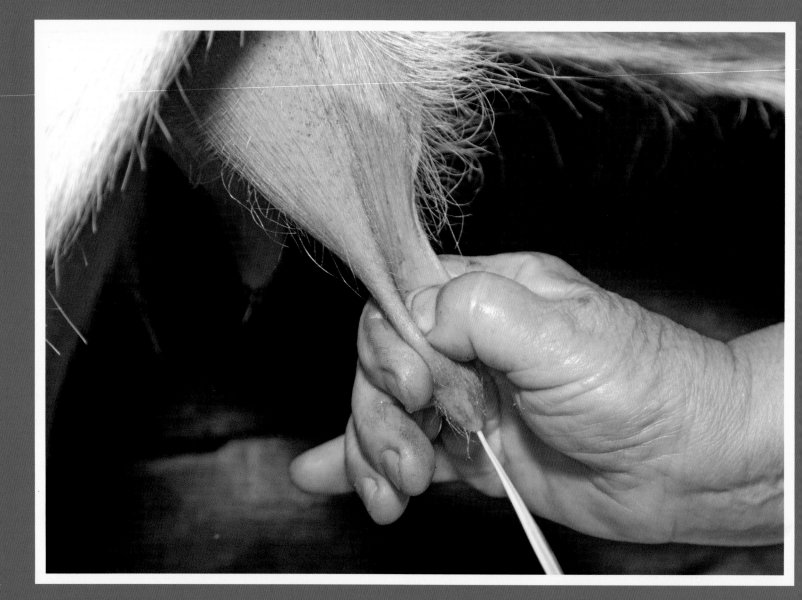

A farmer milks a goat.

SAY "CHEESE!"

Each day, Matt milks the does. While Matt is milking, Alice brings the goats seaweed to eat. The seaweed helps the goats stay healthy.

Many people like to drink goats' milk. It looks and tastes a lot like cows' milk.

Goats' milk is used to make cheese, yogurt, and butter, too. Some people like goat cheese on a cracker.

MANY KINDS OF GOATS

Not all goats are the same. There are many different **breeds** of goats. French Alpine is one type of breed. Each breed provides different products for people. Which breed do you like best?

Angora , wool

20

Boer,
meat

French Alpine,
milk

Pygmy,
meat and milk

21

LIFE CYCLE OF A GOAT

1. A female goat may give birth to one, two, three, or even four kids at once.

Kids drink their mother's milk.

2. A one-year-old goat is called a **yearling**.

3. Goats are full-grown by two to three years. A goat may live 15 to 18 years.

LEARN MORE

BOOKS

Macken, JoAnn Early. *Goats*. New York: Weekly Reader Early
  Learning, 2010.

Mercer, Abbie. *Goats on a Farm*. New York: Rosen Publishing, 2010.

Nelson, Robin. *Goats*. Minneapolis, Minn.: Lerner Publishing
  Group, 2009.

WEB SITES

Kids Farm. *Farm Animals*.
http://www.kidsfarm.com/farm.htm

Smithsonian National Zoological Park. *Kids' Farm*.
http://www.nationalzoo.si.edu/Animals/KidsFarm/IntheBarn

INDEX

Enslow Elementary, an imprint of Enslow Publishers, Inc.
Enslow Elementary® is a registered trademark of Enslow Publishers, Inc.

Copyright © 2013 by Chana Stiefel

Library of Congress Cataloging-in-Publication Data

Stiefel, Chana, 1968-
    Goats on the family farm / Chana Stiefel.
        p. cm. — (Animals on the family farm)
    Summary: "An introduction to life on a farm for early readers. Find out what a goat
eats, where it lives, and how goat's milk can be made into cheese"—Provided by
publisher.
    Includes index.
    ISBN 978-0-7660-4206-3
    1. Goats—Juvenile literature. I. Title. II. Series: Animals on the family farm.
    SF383.35.S74 2013
    636.3'9—dc23
                            2012028802
Future editions:
Paperback ISBN: 978-1-4644-0355-2
EPUB ISBN: 978-1-4645-1196-7
Single-User ISBN: 978-1-4646-1196-4
Multi-User ISBN: 978-0-7660-5828-6

Printed in China
012013 Leo Paper Group, Heshan City, Guangdong, China
10 9 8 7 6 5 4 3 2 1

To Our Readers: We have done our best to make sure all Internet Addresses in this book were active and appropriate when we went to press. However, the author and the publisher have no control over and assume no liability for the material available on those Internet sites or on other Web sites they may link to. Any comments or suggestions can be sent by e-mail to comments@enslow.com or to the address on the back cover.

Photo Credits: © Algost/Fotolia.com, p. 14; BORSEV/Photos.com, p. 22 (kid); Daniel MAR/Photos.com, p. 20; Dimitar Marinov/Photos.com, p. 22 (adult); Erik van den Elsen/Photos.com, p. 13; Howling Wolf Farm, pp. 6, 7; @ iStockphoto.com/onebluelight, p. 19; Jakub Niezabitowski/Photos.com, p. 2; Perry Watson/Photos.com, p. 21 (Boer); Shutterstock.com, pp. 1, 3, 4–5, 8, 9, 10, 11, 12, 15, 16, 17, 18, 21 (pygmy, French Alpine), 22 (yearling).

Cover Photograph: Shutterstock.com

A note from Matt and Tara of Howling Wolf Farm: Howling Wolf Farm grows vital food to feed individuals and families. Products include vegetables, dry beans and grains, dairy, beef, eggs, chicken, lamb, and pork. We work in partnership with nature and people to grow vibrant, abundant food. We farm with an intention of creating a farm and food to bring health, vitality, and enjoyment to our complete beings and the land. We focus on heirloom and open-pollinated varieties, heritage breeds, and wild foods.

Series Science Consultant:
Dana Palmer
Sr. Extension Associate/4-H Youth Outreach
Department of Animal Science
Cornell University
Ithaca, NY

Series Literacy Consultant:
Allan A. De Fina, Ph.D.
Past President of the New Jersey
    Reading Association
Dean of the College of Education
New Jersey City University
Jersey City, NJ